Ronald Reagan
_in_
MOVIE AMERICA

Ronald Reagan in MOVIE AMERICA

A JULES FEIFFER PRODUCTION

Andrews and McMeel
A Universal Press Syndicate Company
Kansas City • New York

ISBN: 0-8362-1829-9

Library of Congress Catalog Card Number: 87-73255

Foreword

So what do I do now? Ronald Reagan has been my muse, the man on the white Cadillac, the true believer/deceiver, the smiling meanie, the happy Cold-Warrior, not just a popular president but a Pop President, our first media president, *my* best president since Nixon. A disaster for the country perhaps, but what about me? I have had eight years of cartoon bliss and now—and now—stop the clock! This is heartbreak!

Political cartoonists have an ethical problem. What is good for us is bad for the country. What brightens our day may spell ruin, doom, and gloom for the majority of our readers. We have a professional stake in disliking our subject matter. It pays the rent; it sends our kids to college. We take a perverse pleasure in *not* having freedom of choice. We are unique among artists in that our subjects are elected.

Ronald Reagan did not run for president as a politician; he ran as a metaphor. He ran as the personification of a system of values that many thought this country had lost or outgrown. He ran less as a movie star than as a symbolic stand-in for movies themselves: *old* movies. Black and white movies of small town America that put forth an image of grit and pluck and goodness and warmth and moral and spiritual sustenance within the bosom of the family, the God-fearing, buoyant, eternally optimistic family.

I grew up with movies. I adore movies. At times, I write movies. But I never believed that movies would be elected to high office, or that movies would become our way of life, our vision of how it ought to be. I certainly never believed that movies would be installed as a form of government.

Ronald Reagan was elected because we were feeling bad. Reagan was elected to make us feel better. Reagan was elected as an ice cream cone. And as an ice cream cone he filled a need. He spoke for a class of people, the scared American middle class, which was fast losing faith in itself, which had begun to question in the late seventies and eighties a principle which it never believed would be in doubt again—its basic right to a secure and prosperous existence, to a life without inordinate fear or worry.

This new middle class which had emerged only since World War II now saw signs of slippage. It imagined what was previously unimaginable, that it might actually fall back into the state its parents' generation had struggled up from.

And so after four years of Jimmy Carter, who offered piety and when that didn't work offered malaise, Americans took a soft-focus look at Ronald Reagan. And why not? Reagan offered hope. Not real hope but, rather, a photo montage of hope.

Cut out big spending, said Reagan, and there will be hope. Cut down on welfare and food stamps and housing programs and there will be hope. Get those blacks and Hispanics off your backs—his euphemism was "big government"—and there will be hope.

And thus it was that Ronald Reagan rode out of the West, seeming very much the image of Jimmy Stewart or Henry Fonda, folk heroes out of our movie past. Until he opened his mouth and what came out were lines written for the mean banker: Reagan standing tall, not just against the Russians, but against other Americans—or immigrants—whose image did not conform to the 1940s' black-and-white movie sensibility that came to inhabit the White House.

Movie-America: Small frame houses on shady-laned streets. White folks with white picket fences and white values. Large, no-nonsense colored maids occupying all kitchens. Big bluff Irish cops standing on all street corners. Movie-America has good safe schools that field strong teams and hold great proms. And on Sundays the citizens of Movie-America pour out of their white picket-fenced houses and parade down their tree-lined streets to attend movie-church, where they listen to movie-sermons, the sort of sermon that Ronald Reagan, a regular movie-churchgoer if not a real-life churchgoer, listened to as gospel, listened and absorbed the values, the morals, the built-in biases, false assumptions, and sophistries.

Ronald Reagan came to political maturity in a world—Movie-World—where Walt Disney died for our sins and the Gipper was God's messenger, a symbol today of nostalgia that the president and his supporters mistake for principle, fairy tales they mistake for reality, racism they mistake for equal opportunity, criminal acts they mistake for acts of patriotism.

Reagan's presidency has been extraordinary, not only for what he's accomplished in office, but for how effortlessly he's been able to get away with it. Reagan may have been a Teflon president but, more importantly, he has presided over a Teflon electorate who, until the day it learned that he had gone to bed with the Ayatollah, didn't care what he did as long as he grinned at America while doing it.

The truly surprising aspect of the Iran-contra scandal is not that our president farmed out foreign policy to a covert junta of the far right, but that we didn't immediately forgive him for it.

After all, there was nothing new in Reagan's deceiving, distorting, and lying to us. In the past we loved him best because of how he lied to us. Lyndon Johnson was menacing when he lied. Richard Nixon was shifty and furtive when he lied. Jimmy Carter was particularly pious when he lied. And Ronald Reagan is telling the truth when he lies.

Reagan's effectiveness resides in the fact that he is not so much a leader as a photo opportunity. He exists for the moment we see him on TV and for that moment alone—and what he says to us at that moment is exactly what he believes to be true even if it is the opposite of the last moment, the last sound bite, the last photo opportunity. Reagan has made a joke out of memory. Reality is altered every time he appears on television.

It is clear that without Iran-contra, Reagan would still be the most popular president in our history. And though I rage at his smugness, ignorance, and ideological blindness, I worry about losing him, our first president not to lie out of convenience or defensiveness, but in the service of a higher truth, a right-wing faith that, as a left-wing cartoonist, I rancorously and joyously sink my teeth into.

What I wouldn't give to huddle with the Gipper for four more years. At my age I don't want to have to learn how to draw George Bush or Mike Dukakis or whoever. I don't want to lose Reagan, particularly now that his effectiveness at the White House has come to match his effectiveness at Warner Brothers.

Between Ronald Reagan and myself, there has developed—to use language that the president will understand—a *Fatal Attraction*. It is not hard for me to envision a future, looking very much like the past, where the two of us stand lonely but tall in black and white movie-isolation, perhaps like Rick and Frenchie in the fade-out of *Casablanca*. "Ron," I say to him, "this could be the beginning of a beautiful friendship."

—JULES FEIFFER
New York City, February 1988

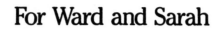

For Ward and Sarah

MY FELLOW AUDIENCE... WE ARE ABOUT TO RELEASE MOVIE-AMERICA.

AS THE PRODUCER OF MOVIE-AMERICA, LET ME LAY OUT THE STORY-LINE.

BOY GETS GIRL. GIRL GETS MARRIAGE AND FAMILY.

FATHER GETS A NEW JOB AND A TAX CUT. MOTHER GETS A DROP IN GROCERY PRICES.

CHILDREN PRAY AND GO TO CHURCH SOCIALS. BUSINESS SKY-ROCKETS.

RUSSIA CAN'T KEEP UP IN THE ARMS RACE AND UNCONDITION-ALLY SURREN-DERS.

BLACK AND WHITE, YELLOW AND BROWN, YOUNG AND OLD MEND THEIR DIFFERENCES AND GO TO THE PROM.

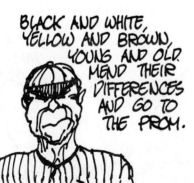

WATCH FOR:

MOVIE AMERICA

COMING SOON TO THE WHITE HOUSE!

9

MY FELLOW AUDIENCE: WE AMERICANS HAVE LIVED AND PROSPERED UNDER TWO BASIC BE- LIEFS.

ONE: BELIEF IN THE AMERICAN DREAM. TWO: BELIEF IN THE SOVIET THREAT.

NOW, IN THE SIXTIES WE LOST OUR WILL TO BELIEVE IN THE SOVIET THREAT.

SO IN THE SEVENTIES OUR BELIEF IN THE AMERICAN DREAM FADED AWAY.

WELL, IT'S PLAIN COMMON SENSE, YOU CAN'T HAVE AN AMERICAN DREAM WITHOUT A SOVIET THREAT.

SO AS A STEP TOWARD RESTORING PROSPERITY AND GUMPTION, MY ADMINISTRATION IS REINTRO- DUCING THE INTERNATIONAL COMMUNIST CONSPIRACY.

SUPPLY-SIDE TERRORISM.

IT'LL MAKE AMERICA GREAT AGAIN.

I PLEDGE ALLEGIANCE TO **MY** COUNTRY.

THE FLAG. THE FAMILY. THE CHURCH. THE NEIGHBORHOOD.

NORMAN ROCKWELL. NORMANDY.

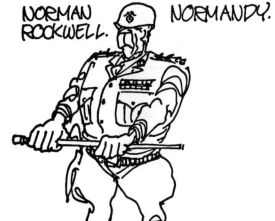

STANDING TALL. STANDING RICH.

STANDING RIGHT. STANDING WHITE.

THE UNITED DISNEY OF AMERICA.

IN THIS DANCE I CELEBRATE CONSERVATIVE ANSWERS.

CUTTING TAXES.

CUTTING GOVERNMENT HANDOUTS TO THE POOR AND THE AGED.

 BALANCING THE BUDGET.

 NOT THROWING DOLLARS AT PROBLEMS.

FREEING THE ECONOMY OF CORPORATE RESTRAINTS.

GETTING GOVERNMENT OFF THE BACKS OF THE PEOPLE.

A DANCE TO SPRING.

BREAD!

IN THE BEGINNING THERE WAS THE NEW RIGHT.

AND THE NEW RIGHT SAID, BE CHRISTIAN AND REGISTER. AND THE EVENING AND THE MORNING WERE THE FIRST DAY.

AND THE NEW RIGHT SAID, LET CREATIONISM BE. AND LET EVOLUTION NOT BE. AND THE EVENING AND THE MORNING WERE THE SECOND DAY.

AND THE NEW RIGHT SAID, LET SECULAR HUMANISM AND THE BOOKS AND PERIODICALS THEREOF NOT BE. AND THE EVENING AND THE MORNING WERE THE THIRD DAY.

AND THE NEW RIGHT SAID, LET HOMOSEXUALISM AND FEMINISM AND ABORTION NOT BE. AND THE EVENING AND THE MORNING WERE THE FOURTH DAY.

AND THE NEW RIGHT SAID, LET SCHOOL PRAYER BE. AND SEX EDUCATION NOT BE. AND THE EVENING AND THE MORNING WERE THE FIFTH DAY.

AND THE NEW RIGHT SAID, LET SEX NOT BE, FOR THEREIN LIES THE ROOT OF MAN'S SHAME. AND THE EVENING AND THE MORNING WERE THE SIXTH DAY.

AND THERE WAS NO SEVENTH DAY.

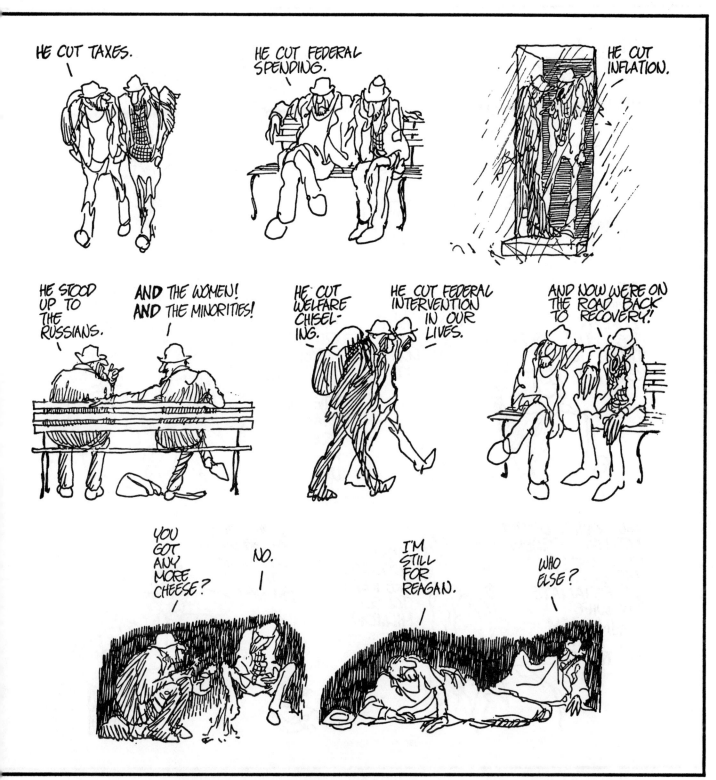

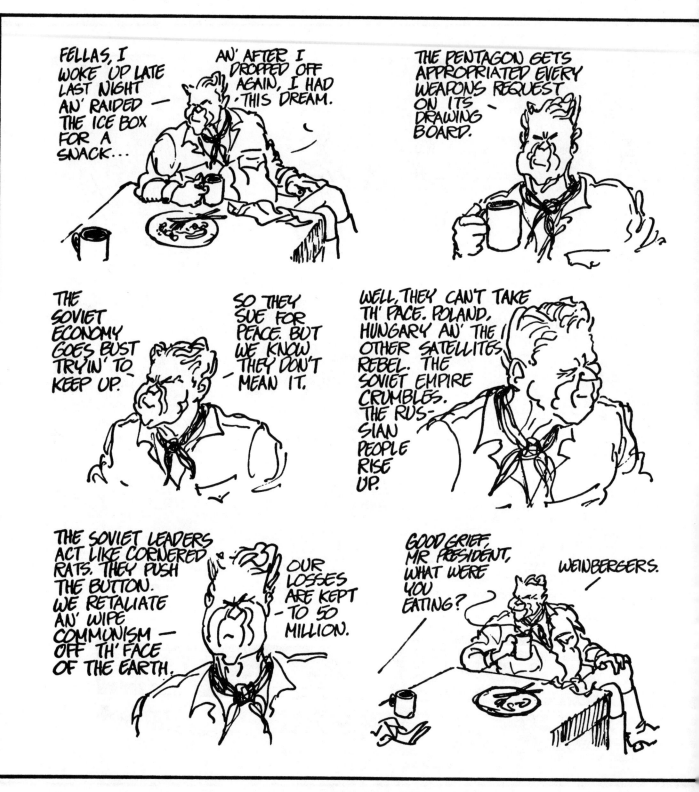

ADLAI STEVENSON WAS A CYPHER AT THE U.N. ...

ARTHUR GOLDBERG, PATHETIC...

PAT MOYNIHAN, UNSERIOUS...

ANDREW YOUNG, INCONSE-QUENTIAL.

BEFORE MY TERM, **NO** U.N. AMBASSADOR HAD AN INFLUENCE ON U.S. FOREIGN POLICY.

BUT I AM STRONG WHERE HAIG WAS WEAK; I RISE WHERE ENDERS FALLS; I TEACH WHILE REAGAN TAKES NOTES.

CENTRAL AMERICA WILL BE MINE; I KNOW IT!

MY VOICES TELL ME.

AS U.S. AMBASSADOR TO THE U.N., ONE OF MY DUTIES IS TO APPEAR ON SUNDAY MORNING NEWS SHOWS.

WHERE I PICK MY INDEX FINGER...

AND STARE AT IT.

AND PICK MY THUMB NAIL...

AND EXAMINE IT.

AND PICK MY PINKY...

AND STUDY IT.

ALL THE WHILE FIELDING REPORTERS' SOFT, DUMB QUESTIONS ON NICARAGUA AND EL SALVADOR.

IF I DIDN'T HAVE MY FINGERS TO PLAY WITH, LORD KNOWS HOW I'D STAY AWAKE.

LEBANON IS OUR BIGGEST FOREIGN POLICY DEFEAT SINCE VIETNAM.

BUT NO ONE GETS MAD AT REAGAN.

HE FLAGRANTLY COURTS WAR IN CENTRAL AMERICA. BUT NO ONE GETS MAD AT REAGAN.

HE HOBNOBS WITH THE RICH AND INSULTS THE POOR.

BUT NO ONE GETS MAD AT REAGAN.

HE LIES AS MUCH AS JOHNSON, NIXON AND CARTER...

SO WHY WHY WHY DOES NO ONE GET MAD AT REAGAN?

HI PAL! MORE GUNS, LESS BUTTER, PHOOEY ON THE POOR, HAVE A NICE DAY.

HE SMILED. THE PRESIDENT SMILED AT ME.

WHAT A NEAT GUY.

WITH U.S. TROOPS ENDING UP IN LEBANON...

AND GRENADA...

AND, SOON, NICARAGUA...

AND MAYBE EL SALVADOR...

DOES IT MATTER HOW MANY MISSILES WE DEPLOY IN WEST GERMANY?

THE FANTASY WAR, THE GENERALS FIGHT IN EUROPE...

THE **REAL** WAR, I FIGHT IN THE THIRD WORLD.

WE HIDE THESE TRUTHS TO BE SELF-EVIDENT.

THAT ALL MEN ARE CREATED SERVILE.

THAT THEY ENDOW THEIR JUNTA WITH CERTAIN UNALIENABLE BLIGHTS.

THAT AMONG THESE ARE LIES, ILLITERACY AND THE PURSUIT OF CRAPPINESS.

THAT TO SECURE THESE BLIGHTS, WE NEED AMERICAN AID.

GOLLY! WOW! CAP, GIVE EL PRESIDENTE ANOTHER 80 MILLION!

FACTS ARE HARD. FACTS ARE COLD. FACTS ARE WHAT JIMMY CARTER — WAS GOOD AT.

THIS PRESIDENT OPTS FOR **FAITH.** FAITH IS WHAT — MADE AMERICA GREAT. NOT FACTS.

/ FAITH OPENED THE WEST. FAITH WON OUR WARS. FAITH ENDED THE DEPRESSION.

/ IF WE MINDED FACTS IN THE OLD DAYS, WE WOULD HAVE GIVEN UP. BUT THANK GOD, WE IGNORED 'EM!

SO WHEN I GET THE FACTS — TWISTED IN A NEWS CONFERENCE OR A SPEECH, I AM NOT LYING AND I AM NOT STUPID.

I AM MAKING IT UP.

YOU GOTTA BELIEVE. —

WHY DON'T THE DEMOCRATS COME UP WITH FRESH ALTERNATIVES TO REAGANISM?

DEMOCRATS HAVE ALWAYS GOTTEN THEIR IDEAS FROM LIBERALS.

LIBERALS HAVE ALWAYS TAKEN THEIR IDEAS FROM THE LEFT.

THEY DUMP THE IDEOLOGY; THEY SOFTEN THE LANGUAGE; THEY MAKE THE IDEAS RESPECTABLE.

TWENTY YEARS LATER, THEY SQUEEZE THEM THROUGH CONGRESS.

TODAY WE HAVE DEMOCRATS, WE HAVE LIBERALS...

WHAT WE DON'T HAVE IS A LEFT.

SO LIBERALS ARE STUCK WITH THEIR OWN IDEAS.

SO?

REAGAN TRIUMPHS.

THERE IS NATIONAL DEFENSE. NATIONAL DEFENSE IS GOOD.

THEN THERE IS **MORE** NATIONAL DEFENSE. **MORE** NATIONAL DEFENSE IS **BETTER**.

NATIONAL DEFENSE PROTECTS US FROM OUR ENEMIES. **MORE** NATIONAL DEFENSE PROTECTS US FROM OUR ECONOMY.

MORE NATIONAL DEFENSE MAKES **MORE** JOBS FOR **MORE** SCIENTISTS, **MORE** ENGINEERS AND **MORE** TECHNICIANS TO CREATE **MORE** WEAPONS.

ALSO, **MORE** NATIONAL DEFENSE MAKES **MORE** JOBS FOR **MORE** LOBBYISTS AND P.R. MEN TO PROMOTE **MORE** INSECURITY TO GOAD US TO INVEST IN EVEN **MORE** NATIONAL DEFENSE.

EVEN MORE NATIONAL DEFENSE IS A CORNUCOPIA OF WEALTH FOR WAR-NUTS BEYOND A PLUTOCRAT'S WILDEST DREAMS.

SUPPORT MY WILDEST DREAMS.

WHERE DO I SIGN?

I LICKED
INFLATION...

BY PUTTING
PEOPLE
OUT OF
WORK...

NONE OF WHOM
I KNOW
PERSONALLY.

THE ONES I
DO KNOW
PERSONALLY...

ARE GETTING
RICHER THAN
EVER.

RECOVERY!

MY AMERICA IS AN AMERICA OF GUMPTION AN' SELF-HELP AN' SELF-RESPECT AN' NO-NONSENSE.

MY AMERICA IS AN AMERICA OF SMALL TOWNS WITH CORNER DRUG STORES AN' SODA FOUNTAINS WHERE TH' KIDS GO T'HANG OUT AFTER SCHOOL.

MY AMERICA IS AN AMERICA OF MOMS BAKIN' IN TH' KITCHEN AN' DADS WORKIN' IN TH' CORNER GAS STATION OR TH' CORNER SMALL PARTS PLANT OR TH' CORNER FACTORY.

MY AMERICA IS AN AMERICA WHERE WHITE AN' BLACK AN' BROWN FOLKS BURY TH' HATCHETS —

SO'S WE C'N ALL LIVE IN FRAME HOUSES WITH WHITE PICKET FENCES ON SHADY LANED STREETS.

MY AMERICA IS AN AMERICA WHERE TH' CIA AN' FBI BUG AN' SPY ON OTHER AMERICANS— TO KEEP AMERICA MY AMERICA.

A DANCE TO SPRING. — IN THIS DANCE I CELEBRATE THE COMING PRESIDENTIAL ELECTION.

A DANCE TO NEW BEGINNINGS.

NEW IDEAS.

NEW OVER-SIMPLIFICATIONS. NEW CLICHES.

NEW LIES.

NEW BETRAYALS.

A DANCE TO RONALD REAGAN AND WHAT'S-HIS-FACE.

REAGAN HAS PROVEN ONE THING:

HE'S NOT QUALIFIED TO BE PRESIDENT.

AND MONDALE ISN'T QUALIFIED TO BE PRESIDENT.

AND HART ISN'T QUALIFIED TO BE PRESIDENT.

AND JACKSON ISN'T QUALIFIED TO BE PRESIDENT.

IN A DICTATORSHIP, THROUGH A PROCESS OF TERROR, MANIPULATION AND MURDER— THE MOST QUALIFIED GENERAL RISES TO THE TOP.

IN A DEMOCRACY THROUGH A PROCESS OF OPEN DEBATE AND FREE ELECTIONS, NO ONE QUALIFIED RISES TO THE TOP.

HOW MUCH MORE IRONY CAN AMERICA STAND AND SURVIVE?

PRESIDENT MONDALE. **PRESIDENT** MONDALE. PRESIDEUT **MONDALE.**

IT DOESN'T SOUND RIGHT TO ME.

BUT **PRESIDENT** REAGAN SOUNDS JUST AS WRONG —

AND PRESIDEUT CARTER SOUNDED WRONG. —

— AND PRESIDEUT FORD SOUNDED WRONG AND PRES-IDEUT NIXON AND PRESIDEUT JOHNSON.

— AND PRESIDEUT KENNEDY AND PRESIDEUT EISENHOWER AND PRESIDEUT TRUMAN SOUNDED WRONG. —

PRESIDENT ROOSEVELT.

— THE LAST TIME A PRESIDENT SOUNDED RIGHT WAS WHEN I WAS TWELVE.

THE GOOD OLD U.S.A.!

EVERY FOUR YEARS A NEW PRESIDENTIAL CAMPAIGN.

CHARGES AND COUNTER-CHARGES.

ABUSE AND INSULTS AND DIRTY TRICKS.

BUT COME ELECTION DAY, ITS OVER!

AND THE AMERICAN PEOPLE UNITE BEHIND THE WINNER.

AND THE MEDIA GOES UPBEAT.

AND FOR FOUR OR FIVE MONTHS, THE PRESIDENT GETS THE BENEFIT OF THE DOUBT.

AND THAT'S WHEN I INVADE NICARAGUA.

MY FELLOW AMERICANS...

WAS THAT THE PHONE, PAT?

NO, DICK!

I CAN NOT DESCRIBE WHAT IT MEANS TO BE WELCOMED BACK TO PUBLIC LIFE BY THIS REPUBLICAN CONVENTION!

I'LL TAKE IT, PAT!

THE PHONE DIDN'T RING, DICK.

COMPARED TO THE DEMOCRATIC CONVENTION'S TREATMENT OF JIMMY CARTER, YOUR 90-MINUTE OVATION BRINGS TEARS TO A DISGRACED PRESIDENT'S HEART!

IS THAT FOR ME, PAT?

NO ONE'S CALLED, DICK.

I HUMBLY ACCEPT THIS CONVENTION'S OFFER TO BE SECRETARY OF STATE IN THE SECOND REAGAN ADMINISTRATION!

PAT, IF ANYBODY, ANYBODY, CALLS...

I KNOW, DEAR. GO BACK TO SLEEP.

IF REAGAN HAD A GERALDINE FERRARO PROBLEM...

HE'D DENY THAT THERE WAS A PROBLEM...

THEN HE'D MAKE A JOKE ABOUT THE PROB-LEM...

THEN HE'D SAY THE MEDIA INVENTED THE PROB-LEM...

THEN HE'D TAKE A VACATION TO GET AWAY FROM THE PROBLEM...

THEN NANCY WOULD HAVE TO REMIND HIM THAT THERE WAS A PROBLEM...

THEN THE POLLS WOULD SHOW THAT 87% OF THE AMERICAN PEOPLE APPROVED OF HIS HANDLING OF THE PROBLEM.

I AM AN ARDENT FEMINIST...

WHO IS TURNED ON BY MEAN, MACHO MEN MY AGE...

AND WHO IS TURNED ON BY CONSIDERATE, COMPASSIONATE MEN TWENTY YEARS OLDER THAN ME...

BUT WHO FINDS MEAN, MACHO MEN TWENTY YEARS OLDER THAN ME NERDS...

AND CONSIDERATE, COMPASSIONATE MEN MY AGE WIMPS.

THE POLITICS OF FEMINISM? NO PROBLEM.

THE SEX OF FEMINISM IS BIZARRE.

O BEAUTIFUL FOR SPECIOUS — SKIES

O'ER RIGHT WING WAVES INANE

O'ER PURPLE PROSE OF SOPHISTRY

ACROSS THE MUTED PAIN —

AMEREAGAN, AMEREAGAN

FALWELL AND HELMS AND ME

WE'LL DROWN OUR GOOD IN SOLDIER-HOOD

FROM CALIFORNIA TO THE CARIBBEAN SEA.

EARLY MORNING NEWS. MORNING NEWS. MIDDAY NEWS. EVENING NEWS. MIDDLE-OF-THE-NIGHT NEWS. 24-HOUR-A-DAY HEADLINE SERVICES.

MORE NEWS THAN IN ANY-TIME IN HISTORY.

AND I CAN'T REMEMBER ANY OF IT.

SOVIET SANCTIONS DEFICIT HOMELESS CONTRAS PORNO FAMINE TERRORISM AXES DROUGHT

NOW IT'S A DRUG EPIDEMIC.

BUT I DON'T HAVE TO WORRY ABOUT THE DRUG EPIDEMIC BECAUSE NEXT WEEK IT WON'T BE NEWS ANYMORE.

THERE'LL BE NEWER NEWS.

THAT'S WHY I LOVE NEWS.

IT'S INFORMATIVE WITHOUT BEING SERIOUS.

WE TRIED DAN RATHER IN A SWEATER. BUT THE RATINGS WENT DOWN.

WE TRIED HIM IN A PIN STRIPE, SMOKING A PIPE. STILL THE RATINGS DROPPED.

WE TRIED HIM WITH SHORT SLEEVES, HAIRY FOREARMS, A GLASS OF SCOTCH. LOST 3 POINTS.

WHAT IF DAN ISN'T THE **ONLY** PROBLEM? MAYBE THE PROBLEM IS THE SMUG, OVERWROUGHT, SIMPLE-MINDED WAY WE PRESENT THE NEWS.

OR WE COULD TRY HIM IN A DRESS.

THIS IS DAN RATHER FROM INSIDE THE PRESIDENT'S COLON, WHICH IS TO BE REMOVED TODAY.

THIS IS TOM BROKAW FROM INSIDE THE PRESIDENT'S NOSE, A PIECE OF WHICH IS TO BE REMOVED TODAY.

THIS IS PETER JENNINGS IN A SPECIAL REPORT FROM THE PRESIDENT'S THROAT, A SMALL PIECE OF WHICH WILL BE SILENCED TODAY.

THIS IS TED KOPPEL FROM INSIDE THE PRESIDENT'S NAVEL.

THE PRESIDENT'S DOCTORS REPORT THAT LITTLE IS LEFT OF HIM BUT ONE-LINERS.

BUT A SMALL GROWTH ON THE PRESIDENT'S NAVEL IS BEING ANALYZED TO SEE IF HE IS GIVING BIRTH TO HIMSELF.

POLLS INDICATE THAT THE POPULARITY OF THE PRESIDENT'S PIECES STANDS HIGHER THAN EVER.

I FEEL SORRY FOR GEORGE WILL.

ON THE SURFACE SO BRIGHT, ARTICULATE, SELF-CONFIDENT. BUT UNDERNEATH, SUCH A **LITTLE** BOY.

I SEE GEORGE IN CLASS, ALWAYS THE **FIRST** TO RAISE HIS HAND.

DOING HOMEWORK FOR THE BIG BOYS.

FAKING AN INTEREST IN SPORTS SO HE'LL BE THOUGHT OF AS REGULAR.

AND NOW, **EVERY TIME** YOU LOOK, HE'S ON TV!

BUT IS IT WHAT HIS HEART CRIES OUT FOR?

COME TO ME, GEORGIE!

A WOMAN KNOWS.

61

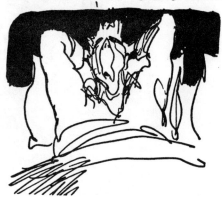

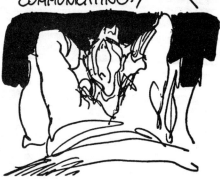

I WROTE A STORY ON SEX ON CAMPUS FOR MY HIGH SCHOOL NEWSPAPER.  IT GOT KILLED.

I WROTE A STORY ON GRADING BIAS TOWARD ATHLETES.  IT GOT KILLED.

 THE FACULTY ADVISER CALLED ME IN TO ADMONISH ME THAT A FREE PRESS WAS A PRIVILEGE THAT I HAD TO EARN, NOT A LICENSE TO ABUSE AUTHORITY.

 "HOW DO I EARN IT?" I ASKED. "BECOME WELL-EDUCATED," SAID THE FACULTY ADVISER.

NOW I'M THIRTY. I'M A JOURNALIST. AND NO ONE CENSORS ME ANYMORE.  BECAUSE I'M WELL-EDUCATED.

 NOW I CENSOR MYSELF.

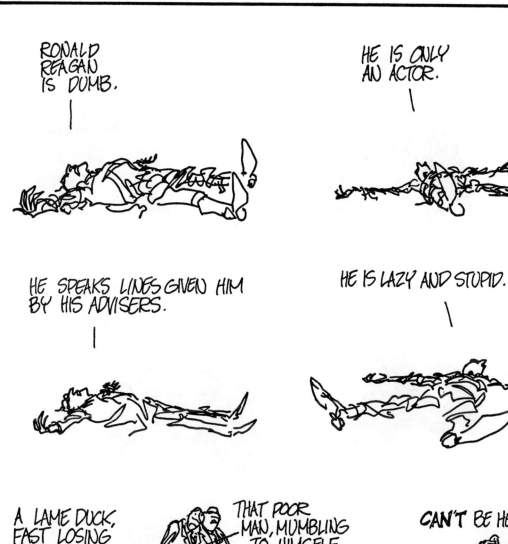

PRESIDENT REAGAN'S BOMBING OF LIBYA WAS RECKLESS AND FOOLHARDY...

IT RAISES THE ANTE ON WORLDWIDE TERRORISM...

IT ESCALATES THE DANGER TO U.S. CITIZENS AT HOME AND ABROAD.

HOWEVER...

AS A CONGRESSIONAL LIBERAL, I SUPPORT IT...

...TO BALANCE MY VOTE AGAINST THE CONTRAS...

SO THE WHITE HOUSE CAN'T SAY I'M A WIMP.

 I WAS APPROACHED BY THREE PANHANDLERS.

 THE FIRST WAS AN OLD HISPANIC WOMAN, AND I GAVE HER A QUARTER.

 THE SECOND WAS A MIDDLE-AGED BLACK MAN, AND I GAVE HIM A QUARTER.

 THE THIRD WAS A YOUNG WHITE FELLOW WHOM I RECOGNIZED AS A COLLEGE CLASSMATE.

 WE CHATTED FOR A MOMENT ABOUT OLD TIMES, AND WHAT HAD BECOME OF THIS PERSON AND THAT.

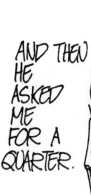 AND THEN HE ASKED ME FOR A QUARTER.

 AND I SAID NO.

ITS TOO HUMILIATING TO GIVE TO BEGGARS OF ONE'S OWN CLASS.

WHEN GOVERN-
MENT HELPS
THE
POOR...

THE POOR
BECOME
DEPENDENT
ON
HANDOUTS.

WHEN PRIVATE
ORGANIZATIONS
HELP THE
POOR....

THE
POOR
CAN'T
BECOME
DEPEND-
ENT—

NOT ENOUGH
MONEY IS
AVAILABLE.

IF WE FED-
ERALIZE
AID TO
THE POOR,
WE MAKE
'EM
LAZY.

IF WE PRIVATIZE
AID TO THE POOR,
WE KEEP 'EM ON
THEIR
TOES

THE QUESTION
EACH AMERICAN
MUST ASK IS:
WHAT
QUALITY
POOR
DO WE
WANT?

A NOISY,
SOCIALIST
POOR
WHO
DEMAND
SOMETHING
FOR
NOTHING?...

OR A QUIET,
FREE ENTER-
PRISE POOR
WHO HAVE
BEEN
TAUGHT
TO BE
GRATE-
FUL?

HOUSING THE HOMELESS

A FREE MARKET APPROACH

First: tear down low-income housing and put up luxury high-rises.

Next, install shops, markets, restaurants...

Then, move in the rich.

The rich object to their view of the homeless.

They hire police to drive them out.

The rich become disgusted and move back to the suburbs.

Shops, markets, restaurants close.

The neighborhood dies.

The homeless move in.

PROBLEM SOLVING, AMERICAN STYLE

ONCE I WAS OUT OF LAW SCHOOL— I ACTED ON MY IDEALS.

LEGAL AID TO THE POOR. ENVIRONMENTAL LAW.

PRO-BONO CIVIL RIGHTS AND CIVIL LIBERTIES LITIGATION. ANTI-NUCLEAR LITIGATION.

AFTER TWO YEARS OF MORALITY, NONE OF MY COLLEAGUES WOULD TAKE ME SERIOUSLY.

NOW I'M JOINING THE FIRM THAT'S DEFENDING UNION CARBIDE.

SO I CAN ESTABLISH CREDIBILITY.

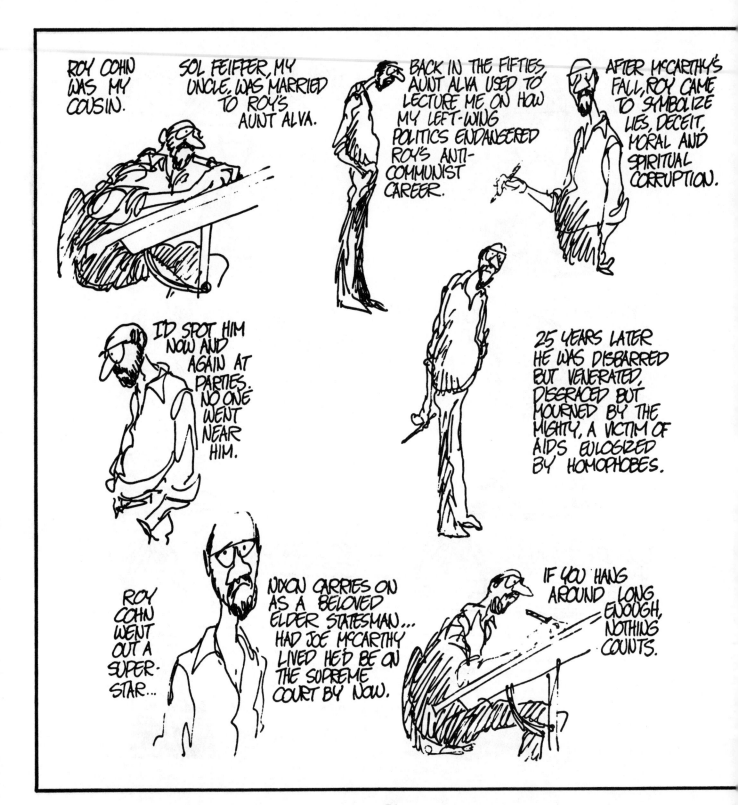

ROY COHN WAS MY COUSIN.

SOL FEIFFER, MY UNCLE, WAS MARRIED TO ROY'S AUNT ALVA.

BACK IN THE FIFTIES, AUNT ALVA USED TO LECTURE ME ON HOW MY LEFT-WING POLITICS ENDANGERED ROY'S ANTI-COMMUNIST CAREER.

AFTER McCARTHY'S FALL, ROY CAME TO SYMBOLIZE LIES, DECEIT, MORAL AND SPIRITUAL CORRUPTION.

I'D SPOT HIM NOW AND AGAIN AT PARTIES. NO ONE WENT NEAR HIM.

25 YEARS LATER HE WAS DISBARRED BUT VENERATED, DISGRACED BUT MOURNED BY THE MIGHTY, A VICTIM OF AIDS EULOGIZED BY HOMOPHOBES.

ROY COHN WENT OUT A SUPER-STAR...

NIXON CARRIES ON AS A BELOVED ELDER STATESMAN... HAD JOE McCARTHY LIVED HE'D BE ON THE SUPREME COURT BY NOW.

IF YOU HANG AROUND LONG ENOUGH, NOTHING COUNTS.

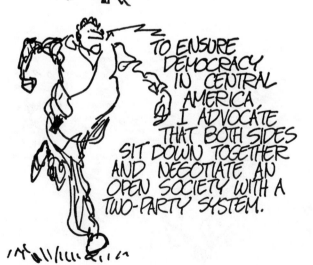

CAN'T BOMB TERRORISTS. CAN'T FIND 'EM TO BOMB.

AND IF YOU FIND 'EM, WHAT ABOUT THE SAFETY OF HOSTAGES?

AND THE SLAUGHTER OF INNOCENT WOMEN AND CHILDREN?

A MAN HATES TO NEGOTIATE WITH TERRORISTS.

A MAN HATES TO GIVE UP RETRIBUTION.

PHEW! REAL LIFE IS HARD!

ONLY ONE WAY I KNOW TO STRIKE BACK AT TERRORISM.

GET STALLONE TO MAKE A MOVIE.

FOR SUMMER OF '86, HERE ARE MY CONCEPTS.

RAMBO: FIRST LOVE. RAMBO FALLS FOR AN AMAZON SOVIET ATHLETE ON STEROIDS. BRUTAL SEX TO THE FINISH.

② **RAMBO: THIRD WORLD.** RAMBO CLEANS COMMUNIST SUBVERSION OUT OF CENTRAL AMERICA. THOUSANDS DIE.

③ **RAMBO: THE SECOND COMING.** RAMBO SAVES JESUS FROM THE CROSS—AND THE NEW RELIGION IS NAMED AFTER **HIM**.

④ **RAMBO III MEETS ROCKY V.** A FIGHT TO THE DEATH. WHICH SERIES WILL COME OUT ALIVE?

⑤ **RAMBO: WHITE HOUSE PART I.** PRESIDENT RAMBO WASTES THE POLITICIANS, GUNS DOWN THE MEDIA AND NUKES ALL THE TERRORISTS IN THE WORLD.

THIS TIME WE WIN.

HOW POLLS ACTUALLY WORK

SOUTH AFRICA IS PART OF THE FREE, WORLD.

THE FREE WORLD IS IN A MORTAL STRUG- GLE WITH THE COMMU- NIST WORLD... WHICH ENSLAVES ITS PEOPLE.

IF SOUTH AFRICA FREES ITS BLACKS, THEY WILL TAKE OVER THE GOVERNMENT.

THEY WILL JOIN THE COMMUNIST WORLD, WHICH ENSLAVES ITS PEOPLE.

SO IN ORDER TO REMAIN PART OF, THE FREE WORLD...

SOUTH AFRICA MUST CONTINUE TO ENSLAVE ITS BLACKS. AS GOD IS MY WITNESS, REV. FALWELL, YOU'RE A GREAT COMMUNI- CATOR.

PRESIDENT BOTHA, HOW DO YOU VIEW U.S. POLICY TOWARD SOUTH AFRICA?

I SYMPATHIZE WITH YOUR COUNTRY'S NEED TO MOVE SLOWLY, OUT OF POLITICAL CONSIDERATIONS.

SOME SAY YOU ARE DRAGGING YOUR HEELS, BUT I AM AN OPTIMIST.

I SEE POSITIVE SIGNS.

FOR EXAMPLE:

THE VISIT OF REVEREND FALWELL, THE CONSTANT SUPPORT OF PRESIDENT REAGAN...

THE RECENT GAINS OF YOUR JUSTICE DEPARTMENT IN COUNTERING CIVIL RIGHTS...

BLACK APATHY... THE COLLAPSE OF LIBERALISM...

IT ALL GIVES ONE HOPE:

THAT BY THE YEAR 2000, THE U.S. WILL ALSO HAVE APARTHEID.

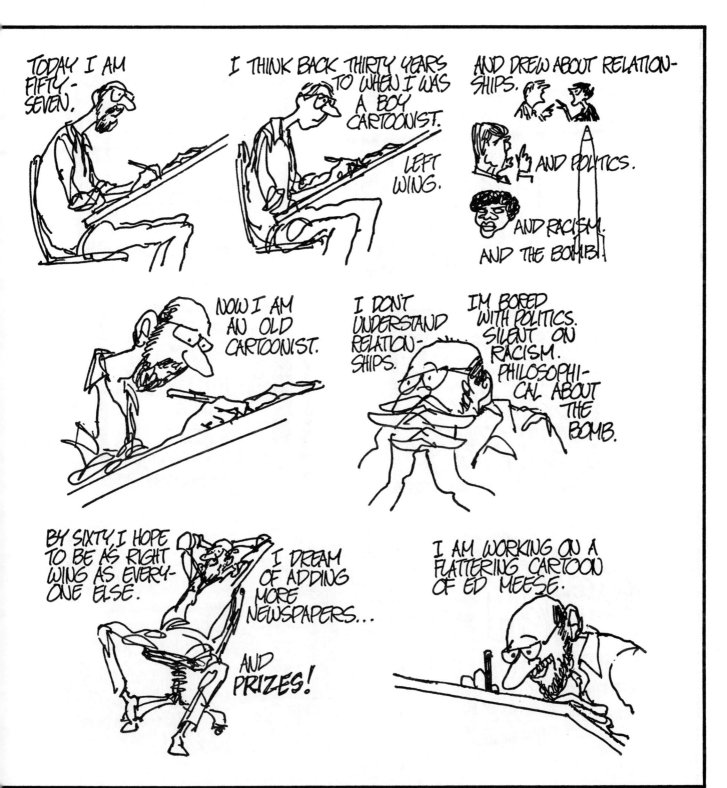

MY FATHER, I BET HE HAD A GOOD TIME AT MY AGE.

MY GRANDFATHER, I'M SURE HE HAD A BALL.

BUT AM **I** MAKING OUT WITH EVERY GIRL I CAN LAY MY HANDS ON?

AM **I** BAR-HOPPING TILL TWO OR THREE EVERY MORNING?

I'M 20! I'M BIG! I SHOULD BE OUT THERE! BREAKING HEARTS! IN AND OUT OF THE BACKS OF CARS! DARK HALLWAYS! TUNNELS!

INSTEAD I'M TRAPPED IN A RELATION-SHIP WITH **ONE** GIRL. *YOU!*

AIDS HAS MURDERED MY YOUTH.

I NEVER DREAMED I'D SEE THE WORD "CONDOM" IN A FAMILY NEWSPAPER.

BUT, BY GOD, IT'S **EVERYWHERE!** "CONDOM."

"ORAL SEX." "MASTURBATION."

AIDS HAS LIBERATED THE LANGUAGE.

NEWSPAPERS CAN NOW PRINT ALMOST ANYTHING AND GET AWAY WITH IT!

BY THE TIME THEY PRINT THE "F" WORD, NO ONE WILL BE DOING IT ANYMORE.

MONDAY: THE WHITE HOUSE ANNOUNCED THE APPOINTMENT OF GOD TO THE AIDS ADVISORY COMMISSION.

TUESDAY: CIVIL RIGHTS ADVOCATES OPPOSE THE APPOINTMENT OF GOD AS A VIOLATION OF THE SEPARATION OF CHURCH AND STATE.

WEDNESDAY: GAY ACTIVISTS ATTACK THE APPOINTMENT OF GOD AS A TILT TOWARD HETEROSEXUAL BIAS.

THURSDAY: CONSERVATIVES DENOUNCE THE APPOINTMENT OF GOD AS A BLOW TO INDIVIDUAL RIGHTS.

FRIDAY: EVANGELICALS CALL FOR CONGRESSIONAL HEARINGS ON GODGATE TO DETERMINE GOD'S VIEWS ON MORALITY, SEX EDUCATION, ABORTION, AND CREATION SCIENCE.

SATURDAY: GOD HAS RESIGNED FROM HIS CONTROVERSIAL SEAT ON THE AIDS COMMISSION, CITING A DESIRE TO RETURN TO THE PRIVATE SECTOR.

SUNDAY: GOD, THIS MORNING, ANNOUNCED HIS PLANS FOR A LONG REST.

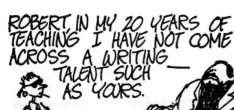

ROBERT, IN MY 20 YEARS OF TEACHING I HAVE NOT COME ACROSS A WRITING TALENT SUCH AS YOURS.

YOU POSSESS A JOYCEAN GIFT OF LANGUAGE COUPLED WITH A HEMINGWAYESQUE SPARENESS.

THE EARTHY IRONY OF TWAIN JUXTAPOSED WITH THE RUINED CHARM OF FITZGERALD.

YOU GIVE PROMISE OF SURPASSING BELLOW, UPDIKE, STYRON, MAILER!

MAY I ASK WHAT YOU'RE WORKING ON?

A SCREENPLAY FOR SPIELBERG.

DO YOU KNOW HIM? WHAT'S HE REALLY LIKE?

1950

1986

HALDEMAN, EHRLICHMAN, MITCHELL, COLSON, LIDDY...

UP TILL THEY WERE LOCKED UP THEY REMAINED LOYAL TO **THEIR** PRESIDENT.

MCFARLANE, REGAN, POINDEXTER, NORTH, SECORD...

ALL SCRAMBLING TO SELL **THEIR** PRESIDENT DOWN THE RIVER.

I WAS ONE OF THE LEAST-LIKED PRESIDENTS IN HISTORY AND **MY** STAFF PROTECTED ME

—WHILE RONALD REAGAN IS ONE OF THE MOST POPULAR PRESIDENTS IN HISTORY—

AND **NO ONE** IS PROTECTING HIM.

TEFLONGATE.

WHAT I'VE LEARNED SO FAR FROM THE IRAN-CONTRA HEARINGS:

GENERAL SECORD IS A LIAR OR A PATRIOT.

SECRETARY ABRAMS IS A LIAR OR A TEAM PLAYER.

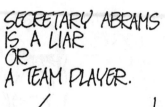

COLONEL NORTH IS A LIAR OR ABRAHAM LINCOLN.

ADMIRAL POINDEXTER IS A LIAR OR HAS A STYLE PROBLEM.

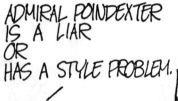

THE PRESIDENT IS A LIAR OR IS OUT TO LUNCH.

THE COMMITTEE WILL NOT REST UNTIL IT GETS AT THE TRUTH.

THE CONTRAS ARE SAINTS.

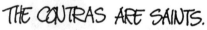
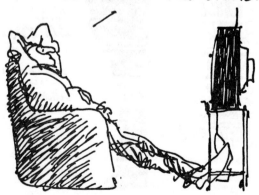

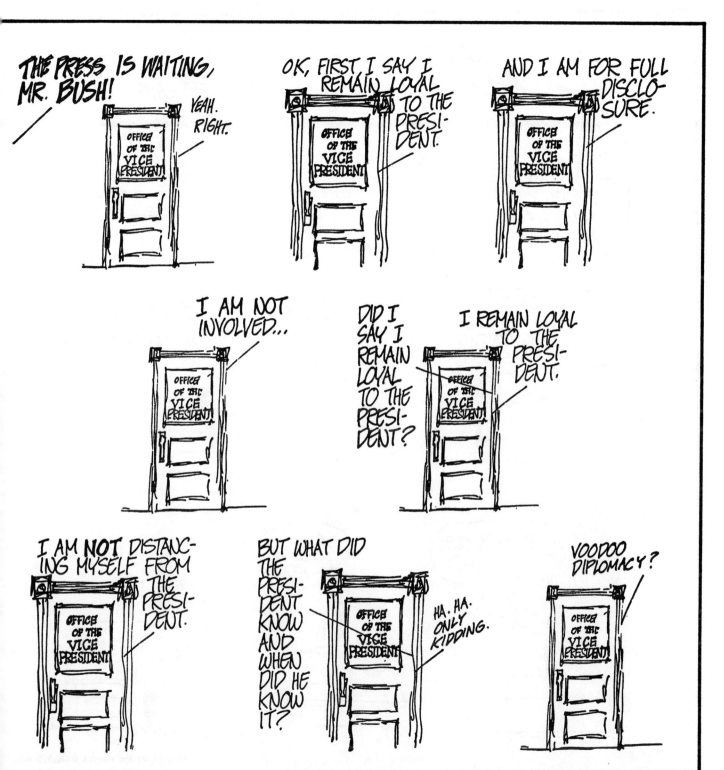

HELLO
DEBBIE—

UM—YOU DON'T
KNOW ME BUT
MY NAME IS
GARY—

AND I'M FROM
COLORADO
AND I'M
RUNNING FOR
PRESIDENT
OF THE
UNITED
STATES.

UH HUH. UH HUH.
YES, I AM
MARRIED BUT
MY WIFE —UM—
YOU KNOW,
DOESN'T SORT
OF UNDER-
STAND MY
NEEDS. OK?

SO LISTEN, DEBBIE,
I WAS WONDERING
WOULD YOU LIKE
TO COME OVER
TO MY HOUSE
IN GEORGETOWN
IN AN HOUR
OR SO AND
DISCUSS FUND
RAISING AND
STUFF...

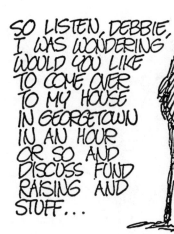

HELLO?
HELLO?

HELLO DÉSIRÉE?
UM—YOU DON'T
KNOW ME BUT
I'M RUNNING
FOR PRESIDENT
OF THE UNITED
STATES AND I
GOT YOUR NAME
OFF THIS
TELEPHONE
BOOTH...

I AM AN AGENT OF A PRIVATE GOVERNMENT...

UNRESPONSIVE TO LAW OR TO THE CONSTITUTION OF THE UNITED STATES...

WELL FUNDED BY THE FAR RIGHT TO ARM AND TRAIN FREEDOM FIGHTERS...

TO CARRY OUT TORTURE AND POLITICAL ASSASSINATIONS...

TO SUBVERT COMMUNIST AND PRO-COMMUNIST GOVERNMENTS...

TO RUN DRUGS AND NEGOTIATE WITH TERRORISTS...

TO SOW DISTRUST AND SUSPICION OF THE CONGRESS, JUDICIARY AND MEDIA WHEN THEY COME CLOSE TO EXPOSING US.

YOU YOUNG PEOPLE OUT THERE MAY ASK, HOW DO I MANAGE TO DEFEND A CAUSE THAT ACTS IN VIOLATION OF AMERICAN LAW TRADITION AND ETHICS?

NO PROBLEM. PATRIOTISM.

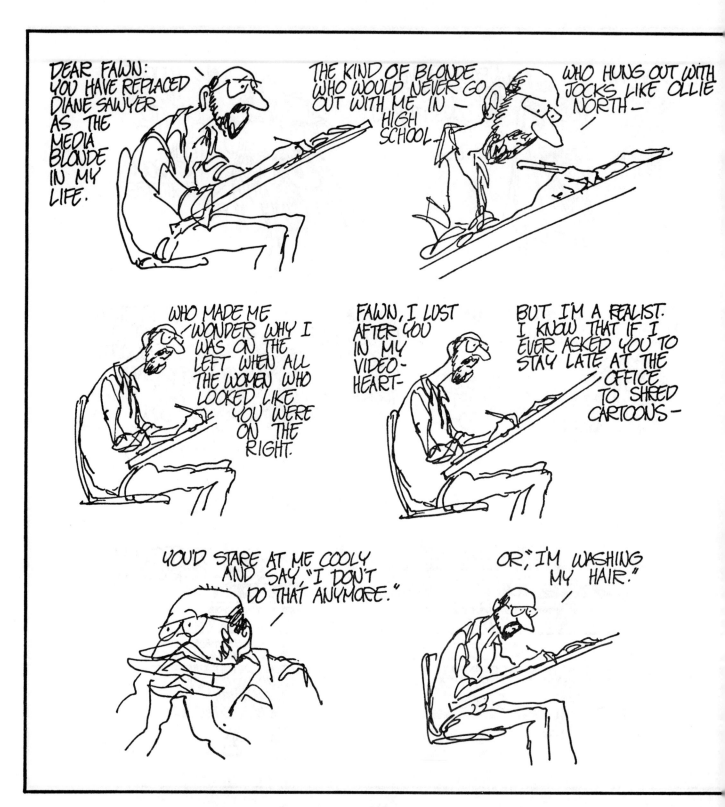

 RIGHT-WING REPUBLICANS WERE OUT OF POWER FOR FIFTY YEARS.

BUT THEY STUCK TO THEIR PRINCIPLES—

 AND IN 1980, ELECTED RONALD REAGAN PRESIDENT.

 LIBERAL DEMOCRATS HAVE BEEN OUT OF POWER FOR SEVEN YEARS.

AND THEY'VE BEEN SELLING OUT THEIR PRINCIPLES EVER SINCE.

THE WAY TO TELL THE DIFFERENCE BETWEEN THE TWO PRESIDENTIAL CANDIDATES IN 1988—

 IS THAT THE REPUBLICAN CANDIDATE WILL HAVE THE **WRONG** PRINCIPLES.

AND THE DEMOCRAT WON'T HAVE ANY.

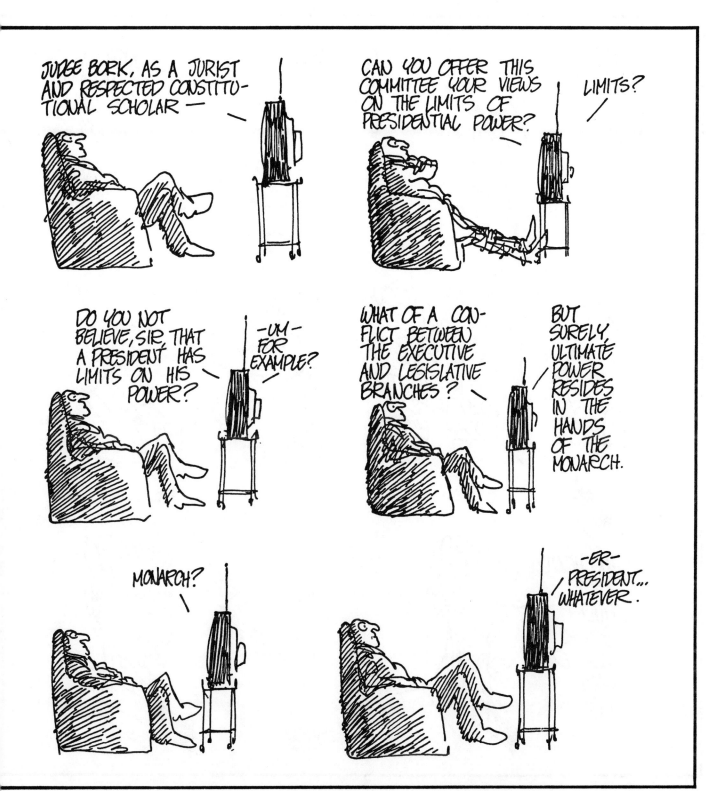

SAM FINK AND I MET AT COLLEGE. WE WROTE "HENRY ALDRICH" ON RADIO TOGETHER. WE WENT OUT TO HOLLYWOOD TOGETHER. SAM FINK WAS BEST MAN AT MY WEDDING.

WHEN THE UN-AMERICAN COMMITTEE CAME TO TOWN, SAM FINK TESTIFIED THAT I WAS A MEMBER OF THE PARTY.

I GOT BLACKLISTED. SAM GOT A CONTRACT AT COLUMBIA. I SWORE I WOULD NEVER SPEAK TO SAM FINK AGAIN.

I GHOSTED SCHLOCK SCRIPTS FOR TV FOR ZILCH. SAM BECAME A DIRECTOR AND WON AN OSCAR.

BY THE TIME THE BLACKLIST ENDED, MY WIFE WAS AN ALCOHOLIC AND MY MARRIAGE WAS IN RUINS.

TWO YEARS AFTER I GOT BACK INTO PICTURES I RAN INTO SAM FINK AT A PARTY.

WE WERE OLDER AND SADDER. WE REMINISCED ABOUT COLLEGE. I FOUND THAT I DIDN'T HATE HIM ANYMORE.

NOW WE PLAY POKER ONCE A WEEK. SOMETIMES SAM THROWS A JOB MY WAY.

PEOPLE ASK WHEN MORALITY DIED IN AMERICA. SOME SAY VIETNAM. SOME SAY WATERGATE.

I SAY, ME AND SAM FINK.

 RECESSION IS:  WHEN MIDDLE-CLASS WHITES ARE UNEMPLOYED.

 DEPRESSION IS: WHEN **MORE** MIDDLE-CLASS WHITES ARE UNEMPLOYED.

 NORMALCY IS: WHEN **I'M** UNEMPLOYED.

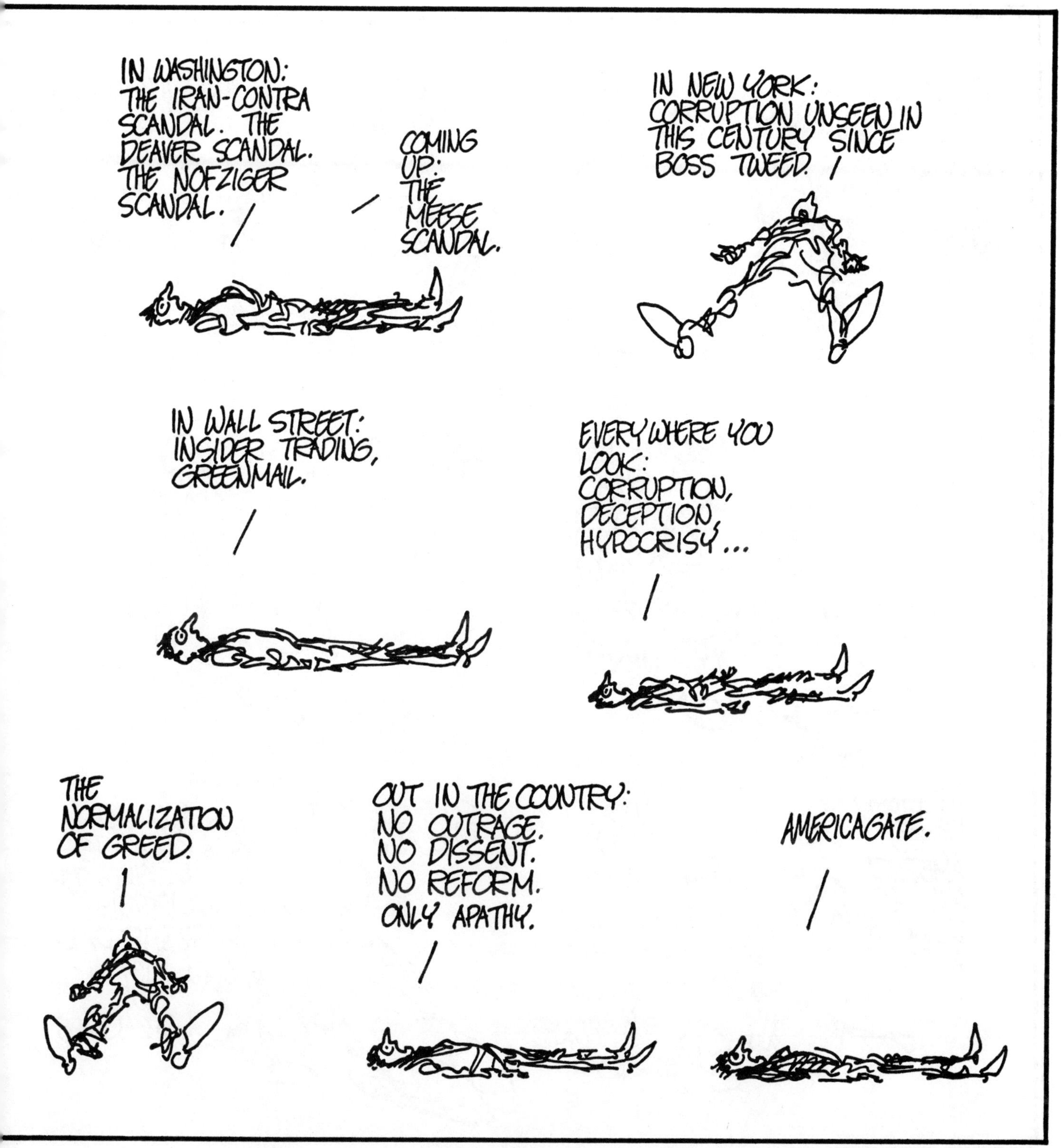

IN WASHINGTON:
THE IRAN-CONTRA
SCANDAL. THE
DEAVER SCANDAL.
THE NOFZIGER
SCANDAL. /

COMING
UP:
THE
MEESE
SCANDAL.

IN NEW YORK:
CORRUPTION UNSEEN IN
THIS CENTURY SINCE
BOSS TWEED. /

IN WALL STREET:
INSIDER TRADING,
GREENMAIL.
/

EVERYWHERE YOU
LOOK:
CORRUPTION,
DECEPTION,
HYPOCRISY...
/

THE
NORMALIZATION
OF GREED.
|

OUT IN THE COUNTRY:
NO OUTRAGE.
NO DISSENT.
NO REFORM.
ONLY APATHY.
/

AMERICAGATE.
/

SLOWLY, CAUTIOUSLY, THE TWO MEN APPROACH THE SUMMIT— GORBACHEV'S DOWN!

REAGAN, WEARING A BIG SMILE, CLIMBS OVER HIM. HE'S ALMOST TO THE TOP... UH-OH, LOOK OUT! ROCK SLIDE!

GORBACHEV IS ON HIS FEET. REAGAN HANGS BY 4 FINGERS. GORBACHEV IS GOING TO CLIMB RIGHT OVER REAGAN!

REAGAN'S HANGING BY 2 FINGERS BUT HE'S UNFAZED. HE'S TELLING THE ONE ABOUT ERROL FLYNN AND JACK BARRYMORE. WAIT! WAIT! HE'S FOUND A FOOTHOLD!

THE PRESIDENT IS POSITIVELY FLYING NOW. GORBACHEV IS SCRAMBLING...ROCKS AND BOULDERS SCATTER EVERYWHERE. THE 2 STATESMEN STOP TO VERIFY THE THROW-WEIGHT OF THE ROCKS AND BOULDERS.

REAGAN AND GORBACHEV ARE CLIMBING SIDE BY SIDE NOW. STRONG. STEADY. IN ANOTHER 90 SECONDS THEY WILL BE AT THE SUMMIT!

MR. PRESIDENT, MR. SECRETARY, WELCOME. THIS IS SAM DONALDSON LOOKING DOWN ON YOU. WHY DO YOU THINK IT TOOK YOU SO LONG?

THERE LIES A **PROFOUND** DANGER IN A LIMITED ARMS DEAL BETWEEN THE U.S. AND THE SOVIET UNION.

WHAT IF THIS OPENS THE DOOR TO AN **UNLIMITED** ARMS DEAL?

AND THIS SETS THE STAGE FOR A DEAL ON CONVENTIONAL FORCES?

AND THIS LESSENS THE TENSION BETWEEN NATO AND THE EASTERN BLOC?

AND THIS UNLEASHES THE SPIRIT OF GLASNOST THROUGHOUT EASTERN EUROPE?

AND THE COLD WAR ENDS?

WHAT WILL MY KIND DO FOR A LIVING?

IN 1981, MOVIE-AMERICA WAS RELEASED.

MOVIE-AMERICA SHOWED US IMAGES OF OPTIMISM.

MOVIE-AMERICA SHOWED US IMAGES OF STANDING TALL AGAINST THE EVIL EMPIRE.

MOVIE-AMERICA SHOWED US IMAGES OF GOOD LOOKS, GOOD LUCK AND PATRIOTISM.

MOVIE-AMERICA SHOWED US IMAGES OF A BOOMING ECONOMY.

IN 1987, WALL STREET FELL.

CLOSED FOR ALTERATIONS

TH-TH-TH-THAT'S ALL, FOLKS!

IN THIS DANCE I PUT ON A TOP HAT, — WHITE TIE AND TAILS.

AND PRETEND TO A GRACE—

WIT—

STYLE—

HUMOR—

AND ELEGANCE THAT I DON'T HAVE.

NOR WILL ANYONE EVER AGAIN HAVE.

A DANCE TO THE LAST FANTASY.

FRED ASTAIRE.